Weeping Willow

Toi R.

Presentation by *BookLeaf Publishing*

Web: www.bookleafpub.com

E-mail: info@bookleafpub.com

ISBN: 978-93-5761-000-1

First edition 2022

Black Beauty

My brown skin is the shield to my soul.
She's an educated, sophisticated, beautiful
queen.
My bones are solid like gold.

My hair is full of love locks and roots.
Tight coils, natural girl.
Sweet smells of cherry blossoms and fruits.

I create art with my luscious lips and curvy hips.
To bear a child and educate their mind.
Shea butter skin glows like an eclipse.

My blackness is sweet and deep.
Eyes so bright as the moonlight at midnight.
Tears fill a river for my ancestors who weep.

Generational curses will not be my defeat.
No, those curses will not defeat me.

Bathgate

Church bells from across the way.
Lounge about on my stoop at Bathgate.

Spit sunflower seeds on the concrete.
Gypsy lady poured out water to move our feet.

Bodega runs, pickles, and corn nuts.
Quarter water, hot sun, and playing
double-dutch.

We sang soft melodies and caught that summer
breeze.
New York born created the better part of me.

I hear street slang, gangs, and twelve blocks full
of cops.
We watched a fight at midnight until she
stopped.

First-floor fight, no more summer swims.
The girl stressed she's such a mess and has no
real friends.

Street lights she fought; fair is fair.
The new girl held her own, fixing her hair.

Bathgate helped me grow and learn.
Legal eagles, doing mock trials, wait your turn.

Virginia bound solid ground, move free.
Street lights were bright like the stars at night.
Created history.

Belly

Summer, summer, summertime.
New move, with a new life, twinkling bright
eyes.
Mingle closely with new fam.
Summertime smell of cut trees, with no city
noise.
We walked throughout the neighborhood; with
girls and boys.
Letting my cousin play with my hair.
Visiting one weekend turned into a scare.
You were supposed to protect me too.
Older family, watching T.V. Where were you?
Belly on, feather scene, he's rubbing on me
slowly.
I froze, not knowing what to do.
Keisha in white was everyone's girl.
Skin black like oil, she was beautiful.
Realizing we're alone, I lie to get away.
Bathroom mirror staring back at me.
Knock, knock.
Is that her? No.
He comes in with a grin.
I turn around.
Sin.
He brings me down, knees on the white carpet.
He tries to go in, baby oil scent.

Push, push.
The pain went straight to my head.
I grab his knee to stop him in his tracks.
Too late!
Warm liquid runs down my legs.
He panics, realizing I was different.
He took my childhood for his own.
I'm left there until she arrives.
A bloody mess, washing me clean.
She's angry about why. Name-calling I heard.
The bloody carpet was washed clean.
I sat in a running hot tub.
I tried to make sense of this dirty feeling.
Skin rubbed raw; fingers sore.
I got redressed and acted as if nothing was
wrong.
I was different now; I felt different.
She noticed I was different.
She sees me.
Belly feeling funny, hard as stone.
Full of a roller coaster of emotions.
Moody, mood.
She sees me.
She calls him over to see me too.
They tell me why I'm different.
Scarred for me, they say.
They plot and plan to set themselves free.
Staircase thoughts, quick blows to me.
I am scared for myself.

He's yelling it got to go.
I pressed against things with focus.
Sleepy, sleepy.
I like her to leave.
I woke up to a bloody mess.
Menstrual flow now.
Clots and pain.
But I know now what they had seen.
I was different now.
No trust, no pride.
Summer, summer was not the same.
I know now what they saw.
Belly.

The Gentleman

Green eyes, old times, gentleman was he.
I ran into you one summer afternoon on 1.4.3.

I was so young, crushing on an older man.
He listened and made me laugh. No plan.

Late-night phone calls asking about who I want
to be.
I fell hard, it was wrong. Oh, 1.4.3.

Exchanges became intimate and truly deep.
Hoping one day our conversations turn into
reality.

One summer afternoon, I stepped out to get
coffee.
I couldn't help but look your way. You called
me.

I must've been crazy to go upstairs to you.
Butterflies. Stomach in knots, I wanted you too.

Your apartment was fly, clean, and had a great
view. I placed my coffee down and looked
around for a few.

We headed to the back where his room was.
He smelled good, and it made me feel love.

He asked if he could kiss me, and I said yes.
I looked up at him, kissing me slowly, touching
his chest.

Realizing it's going far, I had to confess.
I just started my flow and didn't want a mess.

He was a man, so things like that were no big
deal.
He offered for me to freshen up, and I was
thrilled.

He was a man; he was a gentleman; he made me
feel secure.
I came out a bit nervous. I have never done this
before.

Only a shirt on, I tip-toed around the corner.
He stood up from the bed and motioned to come
closer.

I sat on the bed, anxious about what was next.
He took off his shirt and exposed his chest.

I spotted the mark he had underneath his peck.
What looks to be a third nipple, I was impressed.

I was sure I wanted to go through with it.
He pulled down his pants, and he was fit.

He stood at attention, seeming ready to go.
I laid back and looked out the window.

He asked if he could get a taste, not
understanding how pleasurable that was.
I said no, with no eye contact. My heart was
racing as I stared at the sky above.

I could hear plastic torn; the smell of a condom
was new to me.
He climbed on top with his body pressed firmly.

Green eyes, tats on his arm, slowly stroking
inside of me.
He was a gentleman; with no pain, legs wrapped
around him.

Minutes went by with quickness.
He moaned as he ended his business.

He goes to clean himself up.
I just laid there until he walked back in naked
and buff.

I went to freshen up again, clothes on, knowing
this was the end.
He walked me out before we kissed goodbye,
with a cold coffee in my hand.

Goodbye, green eyes, gentleman.
Goodbye.

Monster Ball

I would see you often when I would visit.
Your smile was contagious; my heart would drop
every time you spoke to me.
You had different women often, which made me
curious even more.
I wanted to experience a realness, a crush, a
fantasy.

I would see women come and go at different
times of the day.
I couldn't help but watch you throughout the
apartment, hoping I would catch
your eye.

In confidence, I told someone close, I wanted
you.
I wanted to choose my own sexual experience
and with whomever; on my terms.

We chilled one night watching Monster's Ball.
All of us were hanging out being innocent.
I was hoping you would see me; for who I was.

She left us alone, pretending to be tired. We
plotted.
I was sitting up on your bed, smelling the aroma
of a real man in the air.
While wearing a tee-shirt and panties, you laid
your head on my thighs.

Strokes to my legs while kissing them slowly.
I began to stroke your dreadlocks; to invite you
further.
We made out passionately.

You took your time which made me hot all over.
I assisted you with removing my panties before
you buried your head between
my thighs.

I felt something that I'd never felt before.
It was a pleasure. It made my toes curl.
He never stopped to take a breath.
He grips my hands, keeping me from pulling
away.

Stomach and legs shaking, I began to bite my
lip.
He began to bite between my inner thighs.
I had a feeling I couldn't explain.
It was a feeling of pleasure and pain.

He got up to take his clothes off.
I saw tattoos and a desirable shaft.
I went to service him before he put on
protection.

I got him to lay down on the bed to keep going.
I came up to kiss his chest and neck.
I made him squirm. I found what turns him on.
I climbed on top and rode him slowly.
His shaft filled me up.
I gripped his hair as we kissed.

Hearing my crush's moan turned me on.
The way he stared at me, the way he touched
me, caressed my soul.
We spoke no words as we pleased each other
until the sun rose.

We lost track of time when we heard a knock on
the door.
I readily got dressed to take my place before
anyone else arose.
I laid down where I was supposed to be. Finally,
catching some sleep.

I replayed that night in my dreams.
We never spoke on it again.
I could never forget that night I had with that
man.

Venom

Slithering snakes; take shape in all forms.
Calling himself a savior; by opening his arms.

One summer changed my perception of him.
Who would've known it was your best friend?

Fake sleep when that door crept.
I hated how he made my heart skip a beat when
he left.

The smell of stale beer came from his breath.
Being a good girl, I never wept.

Trips were planned; with secret motives.
Be brave and strong; you're the oldest.

You filled my mind with lies and hate.
Thoughts of suicide became my escape.

My shadow saved my soul that day.
I did not want her to find me that way.

I filled my temple with alcohol and drugs.
You showed me off at parties, followed by hugs.

Videotapes, camera clicks, cats got my tongue.
I prayed to God that I was the only one.

I prepared my mind for what was about to come.
No more dancing free and having fun.

Jealousy when boys would holla and stare.
I hoped for the moment to make you not breathe.
Taking my last peace became the death of me.

One day my bravery began to grow.
I wrote down my truth now everyone knows.

The hate I held for you started eating at my soul.
But karma is a bitch; it will take a toll.

Everything you love will fade away.
Your soul will burn each and every day.

Nowadays, I sleep great at night.
Knowing God is by my side.

Slithering snakes take on shapes to hunt.
But now I own you, guess who's on the run.

Our secret holds power in my hand.
It's funny now who has the demands.

Slithering snake justice will not be jailed.
Headless snake, burn eternity in hell.

Skin

Our skin is not a sin.
It's our weapon that protects what's within.

Our skin is magical and comes in a variety of
colors.
Light like the cream in coffee or dark as a lump
of coal; naturally made.
Shimmer like the Egyptian gold basking in the
sun's rays.

Our skin is ours to protect from harm.
Our skin is supple, divine, and warm.
It complements our hair, so full and yet strong.

We wear our skin proudly and confidently.
It is something others pay to mimic and defeat.
Our skin is woven by power, despite every
beating.

Our skin is beautiful even after every scar
healing.
Our skin is feared and hated by many.

Self-worth is what they lack because we have
plenty.

Don't stop loving yourself no matter how they
say they feel.
This skin I'm in is mine, and it's real.

It feels pain too; it can bruise and bleed.
Lord, stop the hate that they prayed over my
opportunities.

It passes the pain of our ancestors who burn at
the stakes.
Or the overboard ships, murders, and rapes.

We hung from trees, quenching the roots with
our blood.
Dehumanizing sentencing handed down by a
judge.

We grew strange fruits with our tears and our
flesh.
Skin so captivating it will take your last breath.

Cultural passing, bearing generations with your
seed.
Check your DNA because you are a part of me.

Skin is so mysterious it is universally unique.
Our skin is everything God created it to be.

It cannot change; it will not leave.
Not even generations after me.

Confessions

Courtroom confessions verbal blame game.
Some little bird overheard your name.

Tricky questions deflect the situations.
Knowing what we did had no hesitation.

You tried to turn things around on me.
You took every ounce of my dignity.

You switched up a messy transgression.
When are they going to end the twenty-one
questions?

Suits with ties, trying not to be complex.
Jury stands, courtroom fans, I'm up next.

Implying it was my dad to save face.
Now it is my time to throw the case.

I can't believe he is the topic.
That line of thinking is really out of pocket.

Courtroom confessions, dozen was the word.
I see how you twisted what you heard.

Slut shaming, victim-blaming the true gossip
girl.
Felt powerless and unstable like a twirl.

All because of the little bird eavesdropping at
the door.
It caused my world to change and never be
anymore.

A cloud hung overhead, with no more visits. I
am ashamed.
Everywhere I am, they'll know. I cannot bear the
pain.

Asked the Lord, why me?
Courtroom confessions; leave me be.

Mouse Trap

House visits used to be innocent and safe.
I wanted my best friend to stay in place.

Hugs so tight to show you're erect.
Pool table directions step by step.

Cutting pizza with a knife, such a lady, I am
told.
Inappropriate phone conversations, you were
bold.

You gave me new experiences to quiet my
tongue.
Every time I saw you, I just wanted to run.

Overnight stay with her turned into a setup.
Knocks on the door, it should only be us, no
don't get up.

I thought we were sisters playing a game.
Your hidden agenda was unmasked when he
came.

Confused and scared saw a camera in his hand.
I felt uncomfortable and alone, meeting their
demands.
Lingerie and jolly ranchers' photos for your man.
Girl's night with you, no, this was not part of the
plan.

The second time you proved you're only for
yourself.
You both used me and no one else.

You acted all helpful as if you cared.
I prolonged my school work, my heart pounding
with fear.

You made her happy, so I stayed in my lane.
Cringed every time someone praised your name.

You became a person who fought for your hood.
Eventually, they saw you were up to no good.

Karma made you suffer with no respect.
Not calling you out was my only regret.

An angry mob chased you when they found out
about your game.
Glad now everyone knew, which tarnished your
name.

You made her happy, so I stayed in my lane.
You made her happy, and I was never the same

Love Letters

Falling in love with a friend can be the best, they
say.
Hoping this feeling will never end or dissipate
away.

Eye glances and hair strokes while laying on
your lap on the couch.
I patiently waited for you to come and ask me
out.

Not sure if you liked me too since we both are
girls.
Hoping my truth will not shatter both of our
worlds.

I had never kissed a girl before, but my love for
you had grown.
Long-distance puppy love; that my mama knew
all along.

Glad our secret was out now so that we could be.
I'd looked forward to your love letters, not
written in secrecy.

We'd poured our love into letters and described our fantasies.
The first time we kissed in private brought me down to my knees.

I couldn't wait to feel your touch, wishing you would hold me close.
Tonight was the first night with a girl for us both.

My nerves were all over the place; you had my heart racing.
The curiosity increased the anticipation.

Knowing it was the right time to plan an overnight stay.
Who would've thought we would be together someday.

You felt in forbidden places with your warm hands.
Too shy to be completely nude, and you didn't even demand.

You kissed on different parts of me, so tender and so slow.
My first-time making love with somebody, and it shows.

You go under the cover to dive in between my
thighs.
You're better at this than I thought, much to my
surprise.

I wanted to watch you until you were done.
The first feeling of ecstasy was from the tip of
your tongue.

Minutes turned into hours of four play and
pleasure.
Covers tossed not shy no more, now that we're
together.

Eyes rolled back with an arch back, hands
intertwined.
Body sweat, nipples erect, we lost track of time.

Quiet moans, grandma's home, now we're not
alone.
Pillow on my face. "Shh!" You say, trying to
work on my tone.

Lip biting, leg shaking, you didn't let me get
away.
Leg hold, body trembles and satisfying finger
play.

The sun slowed to rise and you finally came up
for air.
Body contact as you gently stroke my hair.

Sticky situations, no hesitations, tasting me on
your lips.
I felt your breast on mine as you passionately
moved your curvy hips.

We held each other close while drifting off to
sleep.
I gave you my whole heart, undoubtedly.

Redressed we were, thank God for that.
The light flicked on, my grandma's back.

Tired as hell we were, but worth every moment
with you.
Now you're hooked on me, passionate looks
from across the room.

Back and forth love letters, reminiscing on what
occurred.
First-time lovemaking was definitely out of this
world.

I loved you for your patience and your
self-control.
First-time lovemaking was with a girl.

Missing Moments

Life of the party, so he is.
Drink to the head, now five kids.

Loud laughter and anger, fist to fight.
React first, don't think twice.

You skipped rare moments, party on the brain.
You down drinks to numb the pain.

Beat her, beat her, cannot run.
Beat her, beat her, feeling numb.

Outside looking in, I was scared to death.
There were no jail visits and no contact.

Priceless moments, you'd biked away.
To have another drink, you chose not to stay.

Daddy's girl hides your stash.
Daddy's girl always lasts.

Drink in your hand; the life of the party.
Another man's responsibility, he's never tardy.

Drop-offs and visits didn't last.
Shooting dice, we did in the past.

Sixteen, I'd become and spoke my mind.
We'd moved forward now, trying to make up the time.

Hoping those drinks won't take your life.
Wishing you we were stronger to pray and fight.

My prayer to God is to heal your pain.
To make the poisonous urge dissipate.

Heal your soul before you're gone.
No more moments won't be long.

Missing moments there's no replay.
You sipped down drinks to numb the pain.

Little Brown Girl

Little brown girl, your eyes are wide.
The world is full of demons.

Little brown girl, do not hate yourself.
For the lies they tell you aren't true.

Little brown girl, you are loved.
For God breathes life into your soul.

Little brown girl, you are beautiful.
For the breeze kisses your skin each day.

Little brown girl, don't give up.
For the no will lead to a better way.

Little brown girl, you are the best, so shine.
For the world is your pearl.

Little brown girl, will you find your worth?
For the other little brown girls are watching you.

Little brown girl, you love your hair.
The crown you'll wear is heavy.

Little brown girl, please love your skin.
For its beauty is the divine creation.

Little brown girl, fight to protect your heart.
For it remembers the pain that you'll forget.

Little brown girl, love yourself.
For it is more precious than any diamond.

Little brown girl, they'll know who you are.
For the prints you leave on earth will spell your
name.

Krueger

Sinister words you spoke with devilish stares.
Hurt the ones you love because you didn't care.

Krueger was not related to you.
Visits to your family, they were my crew.

Girls with mathematical names.
Cat and mouse was the game.

A do-rag and cornrows braids, he had.
Walking in my direction, we crossed paths.

You found the route; you followed me to school.
Sweet charm, I'd trusted you.

Hallway talks under the staircase.
Asked me to go to your place.

Late for school, you made me be.
Clear fluid begins to leak.

You changed your direction when I said no.
Hoping I keep quiet so no one would know.

Your girl, my friend, put you in your place.
I knew you were the devil; you did not stay.

Krueger was not related to you.
Krueger was your truth.

Germany

The redbone girl was new to the school.
Tomboy look I saw right through.

Milky skin with slanted eyes.
You liked me too, much to my surprise.

Late-night calls, we wanted more.
Sleepover at your crib, just us four.

We laid and kissed; I got a taste.
A weekend adventure is written all over our
face.

Phone conversations, reminiscing about what we
did.
Your mom eavesdropped and started to trip.

Changing our paths, we could not be.
Cutting all communication was unbearable to
me.

We wrote secret emails only.
Not hearing from you made me very lonely.

I love you was what I wrote in my last email
back.
Not hearing from you, my heart felt attacked.

My whole summer flew by; I slept the pain
away.
That heartbreak I felt I'd hoped it wouldn't stay.

Too prideful I was, to look you in the eyes.
Not willing to give you a chance to tell your
side.

Walking passed one another as strangers.
Seeing you triggered my heart, danger.

The redbone girl was new to the school.
Strangers, we've become so cruel.

Self-Acceptance

The troubled girl never saw beauty in herself.
Too busy fixing and pleasing everyone else.

She was blinded by the gossip and social norm.
She lived with her truth. Her heart became torn.

Trying to fit in doing what girls do, she guessed.
Going from one to two, her life's a mess.

Punishing her body was the goal.
She didn't want love. Her heart was so cold.

Troubled girl fighting within herself.
Too scared to show she's not like anyone else.

Lust over what she has.
Flirting in the halls was a thing of the past.

So-called friends were so holier than thou.
They tried to preach how her life would turn out.

Going to hell was all they knew.
Baby out of wedlock funny this was their truth.

She's so tired of people telling her what to do
next.
Finding herself was the ultimate test.

Coming out singing that she liked girls.
She didn't care who didn't want to be part of her
world.

Troubled girl, she's surrounded by her kind.
We only have one life, so stop wasting time.

The troubled girl never saw beauty in herself.
One day a girl loved her like a trophy on a shelf.

The Kid

Heartbreak changes a lot of things.
I changed my hair color, mood, and
self-imagery.

You noticed who I was on the first day back to
school.
You hung with a click; you were so cool.

So chocolate, you were with long hair too.
Blue eye contacts, I wanted to approach you.

You made a pass to ask me out.
Everyone knew about us without a doubt.

Locker sharing and walks to class.
Love letters and phone conversations didn't last.

Cut from school to spend more time.
Lying about where I was, I was out of line.

I was scared to profess my true love for you.
Lying is all I know how to do.

She outed your secret out to your mom.
I saw your light dim; try to stay calm.

We snuck around together; we were in love.
But our parents held us back; they'd made it
rough.

You tried your best to be there for me.
Black sand dates and rose petals; fantasy.

Grand-jesters for Valentine's Day, I was
surprised.
But I couldn't bring it home, my mother implied.

The first valentine I had to give it away.
Hoping after this, we could've run away
someday.

Your mother had big hopes for you to live.
I didn't want to be the reason you never did.

I had to let you go, so I got used to the pain.
Selfish of me to try to ask you to stay.

Boot camp you left, to find yourself.
I ended up falling in love with someone else.

The hurt I caused you I couldn't bear any more.
I closed that chapter and sealed the door.

This kid you once loved had to let you be.
You've traveled, you loved, despite me.

New Love

Everything happens for a reason, they say.
We worked together and never spoke; until one
day.

Your male friend tried to ask me out.
Lesbian I was, I screamed and shouted.

My identity went around work like a telephone
game.
You had your opinions about me and asked me
my name.

It started innocently on breaks getting to know
one another.
Helping me bag groceries at work was your
cover.

You asked me out on a date, so simple yet sweet.
You seemed to be really into me.

We both were in an unhappy place.
Break-ups, separation determined our fate.

The questions you asked, you wanted to dig
deep.
Opening up about my life was so hard for me.

I lied and told stories to push you away.
You saw right through and decided to stay.

You gave me the courage to fight my demons.
The love you showered me; gave me something
to believe in.

You gave me a sense of security and love.
You're who I prayed for to the Lord up above.

You were purposely patient with my heart.
Being my hero, you played the part.

Listening with no judgment, you held the door.
To heal my heart, need I say no more.

I told you my dark secrets before anyone else.
You helped with my growth to better myself.

I thank you for helping me speak my truth.
I thank God every day for bringing me to you.

Everything happens for a reason, so they say.
We live that statement each day.

Divine Hearts

Private room for tonight.
Overnight bag and candlelight.

No more backseat rendezvous.
Or quickies in your old bedroom.

Laughter and talking on the bed as we eat.
Grown-up love was all so new to me.

Hot showers, pink teddy, walking bare feet.
Tonight, I'm ready for you to devour me.

Excitement on your face; you saw me in the
light.
We haven't said I love you, but we might
tonight.

I gave a little show, a sexy slow dance.
You were so speechless, gazing in a trance.

Sensual touches as my teddy hit the ground.
We kissed passionately; as we lay down.

You left no part of me untouched.
You took your time with me and did not rush.

Bury your head between my legs.
Trembles, heavy breathing, I begin to shake.

You held my legs, making sure I was pleased.
Adult toys pleasure, you fulfilled me sexually.

We cuddled after so you could hold me tight.
We made love all night that night.

The next night we talked all night long.
When I admitted I loved you, my heart sung a
song.

You said you loved me too; now we're married
for ten.
I was blessed to say that I married my best
friend.

You are my protector, my strength, and my true
soulmate.
The universe brought us together. Who else can
relate?

We hit some rough patches, but we found our
way.
Learned to grow and to communicate.

You're the love of my life until the end of time.
Love is so pure, so true, and divine.

A Poem To My Mother

Fifteen you were when I was born,
Five children later, you're still holding on.

Abuse by the hands that you loved.
Covering black eyes, scared to hug.

You cared for a disabled child; yes, you did.
You put your happiness last for your kids.

Growing up fast, you did it with all of us.
I know you were tired when we fussed.

We took you for granted your warrior pose.
The things you've overcome, no one knows.

You published your first poem about your truth.
Too young to express that I was proud of you.

My love for writing intensely grew.
Listening to your words, I finally saw you.

You listened to me as I shared my pain.
Not knowing how much you felt the same.

Generational curses we chose to break.
Heal together before it's too late.

I thank you for everything that you've done.
For making our life full of fun.

You opened your heart and raised us proud.
You gave us you, without a doubt.

You deserve the world and so much more.
A poem to my mother, for whom I'd adored.

Rainbows

If the world was full of rainbows connecting us
all, would we cross to see what's
on the other side?
If no gender had roles, would we be able to love
blindly?
We love with boundaries, but leap with faith.
We hold secrets within our generations, not
giving room to grow.
Walk by faith, not by sight.
Speak up for the unspoken who are at a loss for
words.
Walk with the sightless who are stuck at a
crossroads.
Heal the sick with prayer, who may have
forgotten him.
Pain has no mercy and is unkind.
But pain is powerless and can heal with time.

Weeping Willow

Weeping willow doesn't cry for me.
Weep down low to kiss that summer breeze.

Weeping willow, I heard your cry.
Swing softly under the midnight sky.

Sounds of the icy water wash on the shore.
This little black girl isn't hurting anymore.

The willow tree knows all my pain.
If it could talk, what would it say?

Weeping willow doesn't cry for me.
I wrote the whole truth that set me free.

Weeping willow blessed with immortality.
Listening to the souls for eternity.

It possesses the power to resurrect souls.
The words we whisper no one else knows.

I'll be buried; underneath your heavenly leaves.
To dance with my soul with your enchanting
breeze.

Weep down low and carry all my fears.
Quench your roots with all my tears.

Weeping willow doesn't cry for me.
Cry for my growth on this delightful journey.